P9-EDR-654

WITHDRAWN
UTSA LIBRARIES

BUCYRUS

BUCYRUS

John Matthias

THE **SWALLOW PRESS** INC.

CHICAGO

Copyright © 1970 by John Matthias
All Rights Reserved
Printed in the United States of America

Published by

The Swallow Press
1139 South Wabash Avenue
Chicago, Illinois 60605

ISBN   0-8040-0522-2

LIBRARY OF CONGRESS CATALOG CARD NO. 75-132579

New Poetry Series Volume No. 42

Acknowledgements:

Some of the poems in this collection have appeared or are
scheduled to appear in the following: *The Literary Review, Ameri-
can Weave, Prairie Schooner, Hiram Poetry Review, Experiment, Dia-
logue, Ethos, Sequoia, The Challenger, Flame, New Orleans Review,
Chicago Review, Epos, Tri-Quarterly, Solstice* (Cambridge), *Ambit,
Mojo Navigatore, Ampoule, Prism International, Stony Brook* and
Sou'wester. "Rules" appeared in *Poets of the Midwest,* an anthology
edited by J. R. LeMaster. "Bucyrus" appeared in the Swallow
Press anthology *Experiments in Prose* edited by Eugene Wildman.
Selections from "Poem in Three Parts" have appeared in two
anthologies: *Mad Windows,* edited by Phil Perry (Lit Press), and
New Poetry Anthology II edited by Michael Anania (Swallow).

For Diana: A Ballad, A Book

I had in my charge two ladies
And I was the King of the West.
I had in my charge two ladies
And two of Angloria's best.

And the wind beat the rain at the window
And the wind beat the rain on the stair.
I bolted the doors and compartments.
I took down the ladies' bright hair.

And they set up a table, my beauties,
They filled it with wine and delights.
Fulfilled and complete were my duties;
Reward was an aeon of nights.

And the wind beat the rain at the window
And the wind beat the rain on the stair.
We ate and we drank and we drank and we ate
And we finished our banquetting there.

And I belched and arose from the table,
I swallowed a pickled red pear,
I hurried as fast as I'm able
To strip me a lady bare . . .

When suddenly face at the window,
Suddenly foot at the stair,
Suddenly sound of an army around
And a voice that split open the air.

It said: I'm the King of the West.
It said: You failed your quest.
Hand over your beauties
Go back to your duties
Get out and work with the rest.

Oh I was sent out in the wind and the rain
And I never set foot in that country again.

CONTENTS

I.

III.

I

Portrait, Room, and Dream
(For Igor)

I-Portrait

He doesn't sleep. He sits.
He looks around.
Afraid of quiet, bits
Of dust and sound,
He doesn't sleep. He sits
And looks around.
He was in love, he thinks.
He cannot smile.
He reads his early poems
To learn his style.
He doesn't write. He was
In love. He thinks.
He scribbles at a pad
With colored inks.

II-The Room

There is no bed. One stands.
One walks about.
A fountain for the hands
Drips water out.
There is no pillow, sheet,
Or bed at all;
A fountain for the feet
Is in the hall.
A fountain for the feet
Or for the hands—
Oh, sit upon the floor!

A yellow needle
Pins a ballad to
The door.

III-The Dream

The King was dead. Earth flat.
And women real.
Beside me Marcus sat.
We took our meal.
"I have his daughter, sir,
I have his bride.
A proper poem, my lord,
Will buy them tied.
A proper poem, my lord,
If you can write.
I'll have them in your bed
Tomorrow night."
And I remember that.
And I recall.
Beside me Marcus sat
And that was all.

Of a Cave Near a Pacific Beach
(for Ann-July 2, 1966)

Handsome lovers know this place
And lovers knew it long ago.
Spirits whisper: love is grace.

I brought my beauty here in lace,
Here to where the shadows grow,
And spirits whispered: love is grace.

Spirits whispered: love is grace
And all the lovers seemed to know.
I took my beauty in that place

As spirits whispered: love is grace.
My beauty did not find it so.
She gathered up her lace to go
And fled, angelic, from my face.

Spirits whisper: love is grace.

Idealism

Love's still
head is turned
away and
sleeping,

Lover smiles,
awake: my
thoughts are
free!

I'll cultivate
erotic fantasies,
huge whores!

Love is un-
impressed.

Nothing in the
dark is dis-
arranged.

Letter

As I say,
I work. I
live alone.

But if you
really want
to, then ok.

Perhaps you'll
bring a radio
or car.
      And
money. And that
lacey slip.

But cut the
giggly happy
bit of last
p. m.
      Baby,
that won't do.

Plan to spend
a week or so,
no more.

Between

Between here
and away
is a
way

and a point
to be made.

what matter
now
is how?

to leave is
to the point

it is

it is a way,

(and equally
the coffee
and the
calm.)

Of: R. H.

(June 23: had dinner with R.H. & wife and kids. Afterwards,
conversation alone with R.H.: he is in love with C.)

A life unhinged — the
stuff of good art. Or
an age unhinged. Bob,
we have spoken of
watching and writing.

But what did I seem
last night? Surely
you knew me a watcher.
And with what designs
on your passion?

I was a spy
for my poem. Have
we not confessed, one
to another, the curious
thrill of betrayal?

Knowing me, you
whispered secrets,
opened the doors
of apartments. And I?
Did I smile like love?

Alastor McGibbon

Should he, if the telephone rings,
pick it up? And if a knock should
come at the door? He ponders, Alastor
McGibbon, the questions. Another
occurs: what if a light should
suddenly flash in the yard?
It is late; Alastor McGibbon
is tired. He sips his tea and
smokes his cigarettes. He
ponders, Alastor McGibbon,
the questions.

There is a light in the yard.
The telephone rings.
There is an angry knocking at the door.

Independence Between Christmas and New Years Day

An oblong mirror
hangs on a nail. Or,
If you will, that
Just and classical eye.
. . . Sixty-six in the year
of our war and on earth peace
bad winter weather. . . .
This, among dishes seen:
Daily news. Also, a faustian fox
of a fellow, fed:
   Below the eye
   A time of adjustments.
   In broken Asia, blood.
"In a cozy room
I'll paint my
beard a regal
blue for the sake
of delight . . . no hand
of mine will end, my
love, my warrior brother,
War. . . ."
   "Is the weather wrong?
   Am I scribbled-out?
   Season of hibernation forced,
   A time for the painting of beards!"
"I, neither
brother nor lover;
no, nor with scorn nor
pity nor illness
sufficient to break, break

open a sullen oyster shell
and shout. . . ."
    "Is the weather wrong?
    I, at least, shall survive!"
Oblong mirror! Just and Classical eye!
Before it now, in winter weather,
Year of our war, he paints his
Pointed beard for delight
A rich and a regal blue.

Thick, Unhealthy, L.A. Smog

I

Thick, unhealthy, L.A. smog. They doused us with a pail of yellow
paint. "No bombs" our placards said and "Peace" and "U.S.A. no go."

II

Paint in the
Eye. Paint in
The ear. Maintain
At all cost dignity
My father used to
Say (who was painted
On a canvas for
A fee.)

III

Paint in the nose.
Between the toes.
And firemen round the corner
With a big black hose.

Three Dreams

(i)
Johnson, Nixon
and Agnew meet
in my kitchen at six.
Each declares he
wants to suck me off.
I'm all at sea until
Daley arrives with
bananas. "I have the
bananas," he says.
Johnson, Nixon and
Agnew peel their
bananas. Daley
declares he wants to
suck me off.

(ii)
The scene suddenly
shifts to the House
of Lords. Which isn't
a house at all but a
kitchen. I'm given
a ceremonial blanket
to sit on . . .
The shout goes up:
HE'S SLIDING INTO THE LORDS!
HE'S SLIDING INTO THE LORDS!

(iii)
I'm due to meet
Chairman Mao in

Hanoi. (Hanoi
is really a kitchen.)
"I have," I declare,
"the ceremonial blanket."
                    The shout goes up:
                        AND CHAIRMAN MAO HAS GOT
                        THE BANANAS.

Chicago: The Cops

reds yip mob
the fuckers
law club
mace I'll
gass she
standing there
her ass &
theirs theirs
them the
country order
taunting fuck fuck
her zipper
sweater tit
she fuck
fuck you pig
says love
come hair
& heckle taunting
crotch I'll
club club
order city
democrat her
shoot hand
sexy hand
and looking
rubbing up
her thigh
her eyes
love love
she says
her levis

tight her
zipper up her
down hand
laughing
dares to
hand hand
club I'll
to herself
inside obscene
she laughs laughs
god I'll
laughing
laughing kill
I'll shoot to kill
I'll kill

For S.D.W.

Animals frightened me then.
I went to the zoo. Like I
didn't zoos a bit a bit.
Suzie led me by the hand
to cage and pen: Suzie
held my hand: Like I
didn't Suzie then a bit.
She frightened me then, the giraffe.

(The Giraffe! Mate beyond a wire
mesh: Prick the size of a leg!)

Suzie said "The animals are good:
kiss the kangaroo and love
the monkey like you should."
Suzie said "The animals are right:
kiss the antelope and love
the tiger as you might."

But animals frightened me then.
When I went to the zoo.

Giraffe would have his cunt
and through that mesh. We
licked our ices; Suzie
held my hand. Turned ass
backwards; frightened me then
the giraffe. Like I didn't
Suzie then a bit.

For M.M.J.

The phone was off the hook.
Qualified professionals
Ignored the trunk. It lay
on its chest. The wrists
were bound with tape.
These men had things to do
and lightly stepped.

The phone was off the hook.
The elevator door was jambed.
Legs and hips lay bleeding
in a chair.
On a landing of
the spiral stair
a matron washed
the head.
She washed it in a pan.

And the manager said:
He tried to get out.
He tried to ring you up.
The phone was off the hook.
The elevator door was jambed.

For Joel Barkan

I met a man, Bark,
who was selling the ace
for a dime
                from street to street
                from door to door
for a dime.
                And Bark,
doubter of doubters, you
wouldn't have given a cent,
you wouldn't have noticed
the grinning face at the pane.
                Listening to the
jazz and smoking angry pipes—
eight years ago he held the ace
and no one knew: twenty dollars
on the table was a lot of money
then and twenty dollars and a
dime was more:
                Cecil Treadwell,
                first among us dead,
                strangled in his Harvard
                dorm on peach skin, Barkan,
                called—
The scene was Marty's
five-o-two, the game was Bernie,
hearts were trump,
and Treadwell, Barkan,
asked to see your hand . . .
                said for a dime
                I'll help you remember
                the things you choose
                to forget

                    Like Treadwell dead . . .
                    Like Treadwell, Barkan,
                    Dead.
The visitation profitted,
I paid.
              From street to street
              from door to door
              for a dime or nothing at all
Bark,
I'm going to start
Showing my hand.

Rules

Simon says take three green steps
Or hang: it couldn't be more clear.

Take three green steps, says
Simon, grinning at not having
Said that Simon says—and those
Who step, he hangs.
                          Hangs them
Understanding that the cause
Of death is reflex, never will—
But hangs them none the less

Gentle Simon.
Simple Simon.
                          Hangs them
All the higher for their
Wanting to be good.

An ordered pattern of disorder
or the knot? An ordered pattern
Of disorder *then* the knot! Will
And understanding have their hour,
But repetition deadens to an
Inadvertent twitch:

None of us can say what Simon says.
And Simon says take three green steps
Or hang.

Swimming at Midnight

(Near my grandparents' home at the outskirts of town, a
stone quarry was established, then abandoned, nearly a
hundred and fifty years ago. The early blasting hit water,
and after many soundings were taken, the management
concluded that they had uncovered a bottomless lake, fed,
they surmised, by a sizable underground river.)

Under a pine and confusion:
ah! Tangles of clothes: (come
on, silly, nobody's here:) and
naked as fish, a boy and a girl.
(Nobody comes here: nobody looks:
nobody watches us watching us
watch.) Except the police.
Thighs slide into the moon.
Humbly, into the stars: Mirrored,
flashes a father's red eye, a
blue-bitten mother's red lip: No
Swimming Allowed In The Quarry
At Night. (Anyway, nevertheless
and moreover: feel how warm!) here,
among the reflections. (Feel the
water's mouth and its hands, feel
them imitate mine: can there truly
be any danger?) danger allowed in
the quarry at night? can people
really have drowned? (Now my body
is only water alive, and aeons
ago you were a fish growing
legs—) well, dust to dust, a
curious notion. But quarry water on

dust green with seed! Quarry water
forbidden on land after dark! What
young forms of vegetation emerge.
What new colors of light.

Fragments for an Epithalamion

Ann, in lieu of ornaments
A wedding song. No angels can I summon
And no swans; no maidens, Ann, nor drunken
Dancing boys. I summon this:

              remembered seas and silences.

In the quiet of the dusk there will
Be ceremony soon and there was
Ceremony of uncertain kind before.
Silent by a silent sea did we see minstrals
In the surf who sang?

             This stillness summons
Absent things like time . . .

             Like angels, maidens,
Dancing boys, and Swans.

To A. from London

Here I am,
young and in England
writing American prose
in stanzas of verse:
                    Hello, love!
Had you come along,
Oh were you young and
beside me here, here
in the garden or over
the wall, I'd hand
you a poem.
                    Folding it now,
                    I'll sail an
                    Odd paper plane.

Moving to London From San Francisco U.S.A.

Packing up books again,
Moving out. Books
Moving on. Well, I've
Packed up books now
One more time.

But not my wife. Didn't
Pack Ann. She wouldn't
Be packed. Stayed home.
Think, think, think
Of her ass
And her thighs.

Last time out I
Packed moving out
Moving west. I
Packed up every book
That I own and a
Picture of Jane.
Jane she wouldn't be
Packed. Home with
Doctor Fernandy she
stayed, with Father
Gonzales and died.
They packed her
Under the ground.

Lonely, lonely, I met
Me a wife, but now
Moving out, moving on,
She wouldn't be packed.

Father Gonzales,
Pappa Frederico Fernandy,
So?

Dust my poem
With your beard.

On My Birthday Near Divorce

"I'm tired tonight."
Oh yes. Or "Baby oh my
back is sore that god
damn back." Oh yes. O.K.
"I'm tired tonight."

And so I spill the thought
of you once more in
handkerchief or hand.

Boys do this.
Longing for and fearing that
initial lay, they spill
and sigh.

In kitchen (glass of
water dear?) or living
room with curtains drawn
I burst, explode,

while you, my love, lie
reading someone else's poems.

Ann, I want a kid.
I'm wasted, waste.
I've neither poems enough
nor progeny
and (Jesus!)

time?

Who Walked With Her

who walked
with her, her
pretty-man,
her love: who
took her out:
who gave her
orchids and who
gave her kisses
too: who smiled
into the stars
that were her
eyes and pointed
out the sunsets
and the dew:
who was her
pretty-man: who
was her love:
who finger-hooked
and fucked her
in a car:
and liked to beat
her up: and beat
her up: and broke
her teeth: and
busted in her jaw:
who bought a chain:
who made a
little pen: who
married her and
marries her
amen.

Homicidal

Zero on ice.
Tire spun: smoke
to three a.m. Hail
and also headlight
dimming. Oddly out.
Weep then weeper,
headlight out and hail.
(Who is now beside
me now and dear?)
Break it (having
buckled) with a fist.
She had cried
for years.

Suicidal

Carpet flames.
Chain grip: incense
in a cup. Violins
and mandolins re-
corded. Oddly off.
Stumble dancer,
rafter slanting down.
(What is now beyond
you now my dear?)
Hold it (having
hardened) with a kiss.
He had lied
for years.

Above These Seas

Above these seas
        how
      simple once was
everything
      and all—

And how acceptable and fine.

      It was a dawning
              dimmed it all
      It was a dawning
              did it up and
              damaged,
did it in:

              Lady, beauty,
              lady of the cliffs,
        (inspectress now? examiner become?)

        Forgive my quest:

                      There was no where to go
                      I was already there
                      I confess it:
                            no greater love
                            no other world
                            above these seas . . .

        Above these seas,
        imperfect, never
        perfection:

Above these seas,
imperfect, never
election:

Only the possible
Absence of fear —
A night of surrender
Without the suspicion
Of murder . . .

      Lady, beauty,
      What has occurred has occurred.

      Lady, lady,
      What can regain can regain.

II

Bucyrus

"Don't do that," said Aunt Ooney.

"Don't do that," said Aunt Olley.

"Don't do that," said Aunt Oam.

Don't do what? asked the midnight darkness pierced by Olley's flashlight beam. *And why not do it?* asked Bucyrus, dead Bucyrus, uncle of drawn curtains and taɪ-papered windows. *And why not do it, Aunts?*

"Your law forbids," said Oam.

"And Baxter rests," Olley whispered. "He rests everlastingly."

"As dianetical truth reveals," added Ooney. "As truth reveals."

But don't do what? asked Bucyrus through the night again. *Tell me Aunts of shadows.*

"Thou shalt not copulate on the floor at midnight," they all sang. "Up Aben, Up Ada. Get up. Thou shalt do thy Anglo-Saxon Grammar."

Olley took Aben by the arm. He had jumped to his feet when the light first splashed on Ada's face. Olley took him to a corner of the room and hit him twice across his nakedness with a short green stick. Ooney helped Ada back into her clothes, disentangling them from Aben's and throwing what was his to Olley in the corner. Oam lit the candles and opened up the text.

"Aside from the broad division of stops and continuants, consonants are further classified as liquids and spirants. They are also characterized by the places where they are made. Thus we speak of . . ." and Oam gestured that Aben should recite.

"Labials, dentals, nasals, palatals, and velars," he said.

Oam motioned to Ada.

"By combining these elements we can define m as a voiced labial-nasal continuant, k as a voiceless palatal stop as in kin, or a voiceless velar stop as in cool."

"All right," said Oam, closing the text. "Just what did you two think you were doing? Did you really think you'd get away with it?

Did you think we wouldn't hear? Bucyrus taught us how to sense a fracture in the pattern even in our sleep, even sleeping soundly and dreaming of a holy discipline."

"Set the pattern, said Bucyrus," Olley murmured.

"Set the pattern," said Aunts Oam and Ooney.

And then, and then?

"He locked the door," said Ooney, Olley, Oam.

Silence choked the room as Bucyrus, dead Bucyrus, shuffled through. *Fail me? Could you fail me? Oam, dearest Oam, first born of Beckey's shame, what has happened here? Olley, pray for us, tell us of the everlasting rest. Ooney, comprehend us, show us reasons for our failure and re-direct our discipline that it might restore the fractured pattern. And Aben, Ada. Aben, Aben, Ada.*

"But it's our birthday," Aben said. "It's after twelve and it's our birthday, mine and Ada's. We meant no harm. We were only happy. Lying in our room asleep, I heard Ada stir. I was restless too, once wakened by her restlessness, and we began to talk. I will take the blame, I'll take it all. It was I who changed the subject willfully from Anglo-Saxon Grammar. It's after twelve, I said. Ada, it's our birthday. Happy birthday, Ada. We're sixteen today, I said. Sixteen years ago good Bucyrus brought us to his house and left us with our Aunts. And Ada smiled. Ada smiled and I knew that she was happy. I saw, though dimly, vaguely in the darkness of the room, that she was beautiful."

"And so you fornicated foully."

"Ruining everything."

"Breaking the pattern."

"Aunts," said Oam. "Aben, Ada. We must set the table. Bring the candles and gather all the texts of devotion and of meditation. Make it elegant. We will discipline the night away and sleep tomorrow peacefully, one day everlastingly, one day with a cessation of all motion, of all which hath the nature of a means, and implies the absence of an end. . . ."

Here, there was an insistent, violent knocking at the door.

II

"Olley, Ooney; Aben, Ada; listen to your Aunt. Listen to your Oam. Bucyrus read us Exodus. Bucyrus read where it says honor thy father and thy mother, where it means, if there be no father and no mother, that an Aben and an Ada are to honor Aunts provided them by their benefactor. Bucyrus read us Leviticus: Ye shall fear every man his mother and his father. Aben, fear your Aunts. Ada, fear your Aunts. Ooney, Olley: listen to a chapter of Bucyrus.

"I, historian, keeper of the secrets of our origin, soul confidante and eldest Aunt, will tell a sixteenth birthday story preparatory to divine, grammatical, dianetical meditation and analysis. Olley Aunt, recite."

"This rest containeth a perfect freedom from all the evils that accompanied us through our course, and which necessarily follow our absence from the chief good."

"So be it. And Ooney Aunt?"

"The Preclear often will require a therapy allowing him to rid himself of those repressions and frustrations which deny a full, rewarding meeting with his auditor. So take him to your room and give him pillows. Let him throw the pillows at a wall. Let him shake them, let him stomp on them. Give the pillows names, and have the Preclear throw them at a wall."

"Well said. And now together with Ada, Aben."

"Oblique cases of nouns and adjectives are used adverbially, and from these, as well as from prepositional phrases, have sprung more or less permanent adverbial forms. These are genetive adverbs, accusative adverbs, and dative adverbs, Aunts."

"Then on, Bucyrus. On. Bucyrus was a large and rather awkward man, and left his house at seven-thirty. He had a handsome head of gray hair and wore a blue, double-breasted suit with a maroon tie. He always left his house at seven-thirty on weekdays, and it took him just under twenty-five minutes to walk to work. He was a teller, Aunts. He was a teller, Aben, Ada. A teller at the Jones-McMillen Bank of Franklin County, and he always walked to work. He always

37

passed the Bennet Bar and Grill on his way to the bank, and always nodded to its owner who knew the teller would take his evening meal inside. The large, rather awkward gray-haired man arrived at the Jones-McMillen Bank of Franklin County some seven minutes before he was to open his window for eight hours of banking, Aunts. His was window number eight, Aben. And there were eight windows in all, Ada. Windows one through seven were attended by women—two widows and five wives. Often, the large, rather awkward gray-haired man was teased by the seven women concerning his bachelorhood. He was fifty-five years old and a virgin. He was a virgin, Aunts.

" 'Aren't you lonely all alone in that little house, Bucyrus?' "

" 'You'll be lonelier and lonelier as years go by.' "

" 'An old man needs a wife, that's sure, Bucyrus.' "

" 'He needs a helper, a companion—someone to grow old with.' "

"At five o'clock, Bucyrus closed his window and left the Jones-McMillen Bank. He nodded to the widows and the wives. By five-fifteen, he had arrived at the Bennet Bar and Grill to be served his nightly ham and cabbage by Charlie Bennet's first night waitress.

"Milly quit,' said Charlie. Her husband took another job and they've moved out of town. This is Rebecca.' "

" 'Becky,' said the girl."

" 'Hello there, Becky' said Bucyrus."

" 'Hi there,' Becky said."

"And right away Bucyrus loved her," Ada said. "He loved her right away, didn't he, Aben? I'm just certain of it, Aben. Up there in our room I think about it often. I'll study for hours and hours, study and memorize until I simply can't do any more, and then I'll close my eyes and think of Becky and Bucyrus: How he must have loved her. Say he loved her, Aben."

"I can't say it, Ada. I don't know. I wish you hadn't said it. I wish you hadn't even thought it, because now I'm going to have to watch."

Already, Olley had tilted back Ada's chair and already Ooney had pinned her arms to her sides. Already, Oam had crammed the

Borax in her mouth and slapped her twice. Then, they lifted Ada from her chair and helped her to the sink. She spat into the sink, gagged, but did not vomit.

"Have you anything obscene to say?" asked Oam of Aben.

Aben didn't say a word. Aben didn't speak, but groaning in the corners Bucyrus whispered "*Raped. I was raped,* Bucyrus said. *Attend to Oam's tale. It's a sixteenth birthday tale for Aben and for Ada.*

And here, there was an insistent, violent knocking at the door.

III

"Remember whence thou art fallen, and repent, and do the first works, and be watchful, and strengthen the things which remain. . . ."

"Coordinate your mind, coordinate the analytical with the reactive and let them merge. Know that the engram contains all passing perceptions, and train yourself to be incapable of error. . . ."

"Realize that the middle vowel is generally syncopated after a long radical syllable, and that it is retained after a short radical syllable, though the case-ending u of the nominative and accusative plural will disappear in dissyllabic themes. . . ."

"Better," said Oam, preparing to go on. "That's better. And now no interruptions, please. And so, Aunts, Bucyrus had met Becky. Bucyrus had met Becky, Ada. Becky had met Bucyrus, Aben. Becky and Bucyrus had met at Bennet's Grill. But, for a time, there was no threat from Bennet's waitress. She would seem to have menaced neither Bucyrus, nor his job, nor his principles of organization. She was merely the girl who served his nightly ham and cabbage. She was only the girl for whom he left a quarter tip.

"Aunts, Bucyrus lived by his principles of organization. He lived by the principles which we have inherited and which we will pass on to you, Aben and Ada. Bucyrus believed in discipline and order. He taught that discipline and order comprehend a here and now, prepare a there and an after."

"Make a life of Baxter," Olley said.

"Make a life of Hubbard," said Aunt Ooney.

"And make a life of Anglo-Saxon Grammar," said Aben and Ada together.

"Exactly so," said Oam. "Exactly so. Bucyrus made a life of Baxter and of Hubbard, of theology and of dianetics, and passed it on. For you, Aben and Ada, he suggested Anglo-Saxon grammar, and we concurred.

"From the Jones-McMillen Bank, then, he went to dinner and was served by Becky. For Becky, he left a quarter tip, and then went home. Home . . . here . . . Our house. At home, Bucyrus had his texts."

"Baxter," said Olley, "was born at Rawton in the parish of High Ercall near Shrewsbury on November 12, 1615. From his father came the puritan inspiration to seek the signs of his election, and later, a desire to awaken the careless of this world to thought of that other realm, that other world to be attained by the saints, by the elect."

"And Bucyrus was certain of his election," continued Oam. "He was as certain as our Olley here is certain. And Aunts, he studied. He studied and he memorized. From Baxter, then, the discipline required to attain another, better life. And from Hubbard, Bucyrus found a way of facing this one."

"Close your eyes tightly sitting in a chair," said Ooney. "Then imagine yourself in two corners of the room. Then go to those two corners, both at once, and watch yourself. In this way, Hubbard taught Bucyrus Dianetics. He taught Bucyrus how to disengage his mind from his body, and how to understand the nature of his being insofar as it existed in this world and at this time."

"And so," said Oam, "Bucyrus studied and he memorized. He carefully taught himself that the noise and the traffic outside the bank was of no consequence. He taught himself to disregard the remarks of wives and widows. He taught himself, convinced himself to will his happiness, to impose upon experience an order and a pattern removing him from all that would interfere with his becoming self-known and ready for the everlasting rest. Any discipline, he thought, would do. Anything to avoid the essential unrealities. To know a discipline is to know oneself, he thought. To know oneself is to prepare for Baxter's rest. And Baxter's rest is the end, the culmination, and the joy."

"A glimpse the saints behold, though but in a glass; which makes us capable of some poor, general, dark apprehensions of what we shall behold in Glory."

"Set the pattern, said Bucyrus," Olley murmured.

"Set the pattern," said Aunts Oam and Ooney.

"Make yourself a life of Anglo-Saxon Grammar."

Because, Bucyrus said from corners, *beyond the discipline there is only danger and disorder. If we work eight hours, well, what then? Eight hours still remain before we sleep, and how are we to occupy ourselves? What are we to do? If you talk to wives and widows, if you follow their advice, they would rape you with a Becky before morning. I oppose them with a birthday tale, told by Aunts, my daughters. Listen to the stillness in the air.*

"Aben," whispered Ada, unheard by Olley, Ooney, Oam. "Aben, hold my hand."

Here, there was an insistent, violent knocking at the door.

IV

"Aunts," said Oam. "Nightly ham and cabbage, nightly quarter tips, nightly smiles from good Bucyrus made this Becky wonder. Lord, Bucyrus was a kindly man. But often, his gentle nature lent itself to misinterpretation. The widows and the wives, for instance. My, Bucyrus is well preserved at fifty-five, they said. A healthy man he is, they thought, both in mind and body. A happy man he is. It's surely a result of virtuous living, they agreed. It's a result of all that study, of that discipline, and of that daily walk to work. He's fit to marry someone half his age, he is. The widows sighed: Too old, too beaten down with work and marriage and death, they thought. The wives thought of their husbands, young and strong. Would they grow old with dignity and charm? Rebecca, Bennet's ham and cabbage girl, had just turned seventeen.

"Bucyrus ate his ham and cabbage, smiled his kindly, gentle smile, left a quarter tip, and Becky wondered. She was not a widow and she was not a wife. She was seventeen, and she wondered. Bucyrus was a handsome, healthy, virtuous man. He was a fifty-five-year-old-virgin scholar and efficient teller at the Jones-McMillen Bank. And he always walked to work."

Oam stopped her recitation to replace a flickering candle. After the flickering candle was snuffed and before the new candle was lighted, in the total darkness of an instant without shapes and shadows, Ada leaned to Aben and kissed him on the lips.

Bucyrus groaned in the corners, and Ooney heard.

"Will you make us spend the entire week in castigation and repentance?" Ooney asked, separating hands and interlocking fingers. "Must you profane even the meditation table?"

Aben dropped his arms to either side of his chair. Hands dangling, he stared blankly into the newly-lighted candle flame.

Ooney placed Ada's hand in Ada's lap, and then gently, for a moment, stroked her leg and inner thigh.

"Please don't, Aunt," said Ada. "Not with Aben here."

"There are certain conventions that one must allow and accept," said Ooney, "before Dianetical therapy can become effective, slut!" She reached for Ada's breast and pinched her nipple hard. Ada winced, then wept, and Aben sat staring into the candle flame waiting for Olley's hand to imitate the motions of Ooney's, though not on Ada's thigh, but on his own.

Becky, said Bucyrus, *never understood. She misinterpreted everything I said and did. I only wanted ham and cabbage, never Becky. Charlie Bennet knew me, and surely, had he cared at all, he might have spoken with her and averted the confusion that was to follow. Charlie, friend and brother, why not tell your waitress of the order and the patterns that our conversations take? Eight hours are for sleeping, eight hours are for counting money out as best as can be done, an hour is for walking back and forth, an hour is for eating ham and cabbage, three hours are for Baxter, three for Hubbard, and in this way I'll be self-known and ready. Ready!–Ready not for Becky, though. Tell*

*your Becky I'm not ready for her. I'm fifty-five and I'm self-known and
disciplined. I'm fifty-five and I avoid essential unrealities. Wives and Widows
and Waitresses are essential unrealities. I'll have no daughter-Aunts to nurse,
by God! I'll need no Aben and no Ada to correct my blunderings. I will not
blunder, Charlie! Tell her I'll only eat my ham and cabbage, smile, and leave
a quarter tip. Tell your waitress who I am now, Charlie Bennet!*

"Ooney," said Oam. "What are you doing to Ada? What are you
doing to Aben, Olley? What is everyone doing?"

"Light another candle and I'll tell you," Ada said.

And here, there was an insistent, violent knocking at the door.

V

"Some nights ago, exhausted from my study, I lay down in bed
and thought of Becky and her happiness."

"The whore, the slut!" said Ooney.

"I thought of how she must have waited for Bucyrus every night,
of how she must of hated working at the Grill. She must have been
as numbed and deadened after hours of serving ham and cabbage as
I am numbed and deadened after three hundred lines of Anglo-Saxon. How alike, I thought, are she and I. Could she have loved
ham and cabbage any more than I love glossaries and lexicons? No, I
thought, she couldn't have. But then, how ham and cabbage must
have changed for her when she served them to Bucyrus. Ham and
cabbage were, I'm sure, utterly transformed into the very means, the
only means of communication with her lover."

"Lover!" said Olley, "Bucyrus who was raped, her lover?"

"And so, as ham and cabbage change, Anglo-Saxon grammar
changed when Aben asked me for a difficult declension. I knew it,
and I gave it to him, and he kissed me for the gift. That's when
Ooney came with therapy, she said, to restore the worship of our
discipline. Olley came with her, bringing Baxter's prayer books, and
she took Aben from the room. Ooney asked me to recite some
fifteen paradigms, which I did. Then she told me to relax and close

43

my eyes and to imagine Aben's face in front of me. She told me I should spit in Aben's face, and when I refused, she spat in mine. She told me once again to spit in Aben's face and then I did. Ooney gave me two heavy texts to hold—a dictionary and a lexicon. I held them at arms length, with weary arms, and she told me I should imagine Becky's face in front of me and spit in Becky's face. I didn't do it, but she didn't spit in mine this time. Instead, she took off all my clothes, and while with weary arms I held a lexicon and dictionary in the air as though my hands were nailed to a cross, she kissed me in three places: here and here and here. I wish Aben were allowed to kiss me there, but Aben, who told me so himself at midnight, had to kiss Aunt Olley while he recited grammar and while she repeated Baxter's prayers."

"Aunts," said Oam, lighting still another candle wick. "Aunts, dear sisters. Don't I satisfy you, darlings?"

Here, there was an insistent, violent knocking at the door.

VI

"Bucyrus," said Aunt Oam, "arrived at seven-fifty-five. He nodded to the widows and the wives, and opened window number eight of the Jones-McMillen bank. In the middle of the morning, Charlie Bennet's Becky walked into the bank and up to window number eight. Becky didn't say a word, she only gave an envelope to Bucyrus. Then she left. She left the Jones-McMillen Bank and window number eight. Bucyrus opened up the envelope and read the note: Dear Bucyrus, said the note. I am seventeen and I am pretty. I can fix you ham and cabbage in your house and then you won't have to come to Mr. Bennet's anymore. I will fix you ham and cabbage tonight at six. I'll be able to because I'm going to quit my job and work for you instead. I am only seventeen and I am very pretty. Becky.

"Bucyrus wondered what to do. He had no idea what it was that he should do, and so at five he nodded to the widows and the wives, locked up window number eight, and left the Jones-McMillen Bank. He walked by Charlie Bennet's Grill looking straight down at the sidewalk, and then went home. Once inside his house, he locked the door. But what he had intended to lock out, instead he had locked in: Charlie Bennet's Becky smiled from the kitchen where she was fixing ham and cabbage for Bucyrus."

Who let her in? Bucyrus said. *What was she doing in my house? God knows how Becky got into my house. Look at each other through the candles on the table, through the shadows that I cast, through the patterns and the order which turns each pane of glass into a mirror throwing back a meaning to oppose the inanity of essential unreality into which I tumbled. Look at each other through the candle flame and ask. Look at one another through the shadows: ask. Look now Aunts and Aben, Aunts and Ada. Look into the mirror of pattern. Ask: How did Becky get into my house?*

"Becky got into the house because Bucyrus loved her," Ada said. "Bucyrus let her in."

"Recite your text!" said Oam.

"Becky got into the house because Ada says Bucyrus loved her," Aben said. "Please don't hit me. Please don't punish her."

"Recite your text!" said Ooney and Olley.

"Becky got into the house because Bucyrus. . . ."

"Becky got into the house. . . ."

"Becky got into the house because. . . ."

Because she broke the bloody kitchen window open, said Bucyrus. *She broke the bloody kitchen window open and started making ham and cabbage for my dinner. I only wanted ham and cabbage, never Becky. I wanted it at Charlie Bennet's Grill. Charlie Bennet's Grill, you see, is just half-way between my window number eight and my texts of discipline and meditation. Just half way, you see. I've always had my ham and cabbage down at Charlie Bennet's, never here. Here I've studied and I've memorized. I'll not have my dinner here with Becky, and I'll have no Becky with my dinner. But after it was over, after it was over, when what I didn't want to eat was eaten with Bennet's Becky with whom I didn't want to eat it, then she raped me. Raped me, raped me, raped me. Right in my own house among my books and on my kitchen table. Forgive me, Oam, daughter. Forgive me, Oam, Aunt. You were not wilfully conceived among those dirty dishes on that cabbage-covered table top.*

"Becky got into the house because Bucyrus loved her," Ada said. "Bucyrus let her in."

"Recite your text!" said Oam.

"Bucyrus loved her. Loved her loved her loved her."

"Recite your text!" said Ooney and Olley.

"Don't you stuff her mouth," said Aben. "Don't you touch her."

"I'll have some Anglo-Saxon or I'll have your balls," said Olley, picking up a knife.

"I'll bite your darling Ada's nipples off," said Ooney.

"We'll have some Anglo-Saxon grammar now!" said Oam. "We'll celebrate your birthday properly with birthday tales prescribed by good Bucyrus. We'll hear revolting histories of our conceptions and our births. We shall judge, condemn, and damn the Becky-slut, and damning her, we'll sing Bucyrus in the candle light and shadows. Rub my thighs and kiss my cheeks, my sisters. Read from Baxter and from Hubbard, Aunts. Give us Anglo-Saxon Grammar, foolish rebels. Come rub my thighs, come kiss my cheeks: Delight me."

"There are some verbs. . . ."

"There are some verbs which employ. . . ."

"Go on, go on!"

"There are some verbs which employ in the present exclusively forms of original ablaut preterites. Accordingly they are called preteritive present verbs."

On a cluttered table top, my life lost all its meaning. I had not eaten at my accustomed time. I had not eaten at my accustomed place. I did not read, or study, or memorize a thing that night. I was ravished all night long among the dirty dishes on the cabbage-covered table top where you were born.

"Aben," Ada whispered. "Say that you believe."

"Aben," Ada whispered. "Look at me and tell me you believe."

"Olley," Aben said aloud. "You can touch me if you like. You can touch me if you'll ask Aunt Oam to end the meditation. I'm very tired. I'd like to go to bed."

Here, there was an insistent, violent knocking at the door.

VII

"What an eternal Sabbatism then, when the work of Redemption, Sanctification, Preservation, Glorification are all finished and his work more perfect than ever, and very good indeed . . ."

"What a life without error when auditor and preclear at last connect in that final ever-revealing therapeutical climax which ushers in penultimate realities . . ."

"What strong declensions, used with case-endings which are of prenominal origin, which involve inevitably the masculine, neuter, dative, singular forms . . ."

"Excellent Olley. Exactly Ooney. But with more spirit, Aben. With more spirit, Ada. A birthday tale is being told, and you must be the chorus: sing loudly then. Sing the text and tune of good Bucyrus. Of good Bucyrus who in saintly charity provided you with what he lacked, with what he needed to insure continual perpetuation of a self-known state of grace through discipline: Aunts. Bucyrus had no Aunts, his daughters. No Aunts were present at that time to guard Bucyrus from all that clouds and falsifies. Had Aunts been present in the house Bucyrus built to wall off unreality and fortify his texts against the wife and widow which he swore all waitresses became, that initial rape of ham-and-cabbage origin had never taken place. We would have barred and bricked the window, turning Becky back to Charlie Bennet's Grill, back to Charlie Bennet's Grill half-way between the house Bucyrus built and window number eight, where waitresses might easily be wives and widows without fracturing a self-known ready life. We would have barred and bricked the windows, turning Becky back. We would have barred and bricked the windows, never to be born."

"Never to be born," said Ooney, stroking Ada's thigh.

"Had we been living," Olley said, "we would have seen to it that we were never born!"

"But we were. Born we were, the night of my conception. And I was first. Bucyrus tried to reason with her all the evening long. He carefully explained that if she quit her job then she would have no money. Becky said she needed none. Bucyrus told her that he made but little at the bank. She said that it would do. He showed her that he only had one chair, one table, and one bed, but Becky needed only stove, and sink, and cupboard. She wanted only to prepare a nightly ham-and-cabbage argument in opposition to a middle-aged virginity fortified by texts, expressed by morning walks, study by the light of candles, banking among the wives and widows, walks again by evening, dinner at the Bennet Grill, and sleep. Stove, sink, and cupboard were enough. Stove, sink, cupboard."

"And a disgusting, filthy table-top," said Olley. "How old are we, my sister?"

"I am forty-three, dear Aunt. Forty-three and several months. You are forty-two, and Ooney forty-one. We're growing old."

"The evening too is growing old. The birthday soon will pass and so the tale."

"Aben wants to go to bed. He wants to sleep so desperately that he is willing to concede and place your hand where you would place it."

"But Ada would deny Bucyrus, would deny the meaning of a birthday tale."

"Ada would deny."

And why, my orphaned youngest one? Why when Oam knows what happened from the first, explains it all so simply and so reasonably, must you insist that everything was otherwise. You, unborn, absent when what happened happened, uninstructed, uninformed by me regarding what I did and what was done to me, how can you reject the history recounted by our eldest Aunt, my daughter?

"And Ada would deny," repeated Olley.

"Deny she may, but she may not resist. So on until we write an end for our unwritten tale of Aben and of Ada, of Becky and Bucyrus. Of Bucyrus whose self-known ready life expired because a waitress broke into the house expropriating stove and sink and cupboard, whose stove and sink and cupboard once turned against their owner were the source of ham and cabbage different far from any one might find at Charlie Bennet's.

"And so Bucyrus died and we were born. Born of a rape which,

48

repeated nightly on that table-top for some three years, resulted in first one Aunt, then two others. Becky never left the house, once, by error, she was that night initially locked in. Becky happily attended to the kitchen, attended to the stove and sink and cupboard, attended to the ham and cabbage, attended to the nightly rape. And while Bucyrus maintained appearances in dealing with the widows and the wives, while he seemed to be self-known and ready to all and any signing checks at window number eight, Charlie Bennet missed him at the Grill. Charlie Bennet thought it likely that his missing waitress was now engaged in serving meals exclusively to customer Bucyrus. He thought it likely that what had happened on the cabbage-covered table top had happened. And he thought it would continue."

And it did continue, said Bucyrus. *Continued for three whole years until I had to steal from the bank in order to provide for you. Three daughters. What was I to do with daughters born of Becky's shame and of my violation? How was I to look into the faces asking me, asking me again and always asking me the nature of their origin with their origin such as it was? Oh, and it continued. To provide for you, I embezzled from the bank and walked by Charlie Bennet's not to stop for dinner or for conversation. To provide for you I embezzled and I walked by Bennet's Grill staring at the ground, walked by Bennet's Grill and walked on home to Becky. Home where Becky waited by the table of my dinner and your birth; home where faces asked me of their origin, where faces asked me of their future, asked me of my past; home where I resolved that the future of the faces was to be a mirror of my past, redeeming me and earning by their discipline my rest. Oh, and it continued.*

"Oh, and it continued," Oam said. "Continued until the day Bucyrus walked out of the Bank with money enough to send the Becky-slut, the agent of our cursed birth, three thousand miles away with still another sister-Aunt inside her doomed to face a life companionless, sister-less, patternless, alone. He sent the Becky-slut away at last, and who would even dare suppose that Jones-McMillen money paid the fare? No one ever did suppose and no one dared suspect: but Bucyrus paid the fare with Jones-McMillen money."

"Taken, said Bucyrus, *cautiously and cleverly. No one ever knew. I planned three years. I planned it from my very fall, planned the means whereby I might attain vicarious redemption. Becky, Becky. Far away I sent you: die then. Die. You came into my simple house unwanted, uninvited. You broke somehow into a kitchen window. There you were when I arrived. The pattern that you broke, the life that you destroyed, you destroyed and you broke with daughters. Call them Aunts. Call them Oam, Olley, Ooney: call them Aunts. I'll send you far away and uniformed with Jones-McMillen money. As a waitress you came in the window, as a waitress out you'll go. Out you'll go a waitress, or a widow if you will, and though I'll not again be ready and self-known, your daughters will. Our Aunts will learn the pattern of a discipline and teach it to their young. Our Aunts are women, and so they'll be, and that will be enough for them. They'll have their texts and they will have each other to examine. But against the broken pattern of Bucyrus I'll impose an Aben and an Ada who will make a life of Anglo-Saxon grammar. Taught by Aunts my daughters, they will make a life of discipline and memory that must necessarily redeem me. Everyone recite!*

Here, there was an insistent, violent knocking at the door.

"And doubtless the Memory will not be idle, or useless, in this blessed work. If it be but by looking back, to help the soul to value its enjoyment . . ."

"The preclear from his corners reaches out to touch the Auditor between her legs. From his corners, from his meditation, from his cautious touch a pattern can be reestablished and a preclear can be free. . . ."

"Verbs with an originally short radical syllable, those which admit of gemmination of the . . . Help me, Ada. Help me say it."

"Recite your text!" said Olley, Ooney, Oam.

Sing together loudly for redemption, said Bucyrus.

"Verbs with an originally short radical syllable . . ."

"Ada."

"No. No no no no. I simply don't believe it."

Here, there was an insistent, violent knocking at the door.

VIII

Olley and Ooney had already reached for the Borax which they would stuff in Ada's mouth. Olley held the short green stick with which she intended to slash at Ada's cheek. Aben stared into the candle flame, waiting for the sound of slaps and gagging, but Oam spoke: "Tell us, Ada," she said, and kissed her breast. "Tell us what you don't believe."

"I don't believe a thing you've said. Not a single word."

"And just what is it you believe?" asked Olley.

"I believe Bucyrus was in love with Becky."

Never, said Bucyrus. *Never did I love. I was raped each night upon a cluttered table-top and ravished of my meaning and my aim.*

"I believe Bucyrus was in love," repeated Ada. "I don't believe a thing you've told me and I don't believe in Anglo-Saxon grammar."

"Then explain your life to me," said Oam. "What are you about? Where have you come from? What are you doing here? Where are you going?"

"I have no idea, Aunt. Can it matter."

"Can it matter?" said Aunt Oam. "Can it matter? Is it of no importance that Bucyrus, turning eighty, found you along with Aben in an alley, cold, alone, and hungry? Is it of no importance that as speechless children he brought you to his daughters, young and handsome then, for food and warmth and learning? Is it of no importance that he gave not only life, but a life of order and of meaning relating you to him through us, your Aunts? Is it of no importance that a birthday tale is being told informing you at last of what it means to live a life of discipline with Aunts by revealing links and parallels from a chapter of Bucyrus?"

"To me, it matters not at all, Aunt Oam. I don't believe that what you say is true. I think it otherwise."

Silly, foolish Ada, said Bucyrus. *Silly, foolish child. She repeats exactly what I told her on the night we set the pattern once again, on the night I left*

the house and locked the door and walked into the snow at eighty-three to die.
She repeats exactly what I said and told her to repeat and sing to you this
birthday night.

Here, there was an insistent, violent knocking at the door.

"And what have you to say then, silent Aben?" Oam asked. "Are you hostile or indifferent to the revelation of your origins?"

"I am neither hostile nor indifferent. I'm only tired. It must be morning now, and I'd like so much to end the meditation and to go to sleep."

"Aben, you're afraid," said Ada. "You're very much afraid."

"It's true. I'm very much afraid."

Here, there was an insistent, violent knocking at the door.

"I believe," said Ada, "that if Bucyrus ever lived at all, Bucyrus was in love with Becky. Becky I believe in. Becky was alive. And if she broke into a house that was in any way like this one, then she did well. If Bucyrus only wanted me to memorize my Anglo-Saxon and to lie beside Aunt Ooney in the night while she nibbled at my body asking me to make secure the pattern, then Bucyrus never lived. If Bucyrus only wanted Aben to recite what he had learned, to repeat upon command the prayers of Baxter while Aunt Olley slipped her hands into his pants, then Bucyrus never lived. If Bucyrus wanted all of you — Ooney, Olley, Oam — to lie triangularly in your giant bed and whisper perfumed, scented secrets of Baxter and of Hubbard breathlessly between the spread and outstretched legs of one another, then Bucyrus never lived. But if all you've told me is a lie, if all you've done with us is an even greater lie, then perhaps Bucyrus lived. I believe that Becky lived and that Becky walked into the house. And since I believe that Becky lived, then it seems to me Bucyrus lived as well and that he let her in the house through the door he opened. And since I do believe that Becky and Bucyrus loved, that Bucyrus let her in the house by opening a door, I don't believe a thing you've told me of my origin. I have no idea where I came from. Can it matter? I have no idea why I'm told to study and to memorize and to sleep beside Aunt Ooney. And I reject your explanation. And I believe that if Bucyrus lived, Bucyrus loved. And I love Aben. I love you, frightened coward!"

And here, there was an insistent, violent knocking at the door.

"What are you doing?" Aben said. "You aren't making sense. You're saying things that justify unending recitations at a meditation table burning candles through both night and day."

"I've said that I love you, Aben. And I've said I choose to believe that Bucyrus loved Becky who was alive."

"If Bucyrus loved her, then what's the meaning of these years we've lived here with our Aunts?"

"A lie. A hoax. I just don't care. It makes no difference what it means."

"Stuff the Borax in her mouth. Hit her with the stick."

"Get a grammar book, a lexicon . . ."

"Make her eat a passage from The Everlasting Rest . . ."

"I choose to imitate the life it seems to me that Beckey led. I'm going to see who's at the door."

"Set the pattern, said Bucyrus."

"Make a life of Anglo-Saxon grammar."

"I choose to imitate the life it seems to me that Beckey led."

"This rest containeth a perfect freedom from all the evils that accompanied us through our course, and which necessarily follow, which follow . . . which follow . . . which follow which follow. . . .

WHICH FOLLOW

which follow which follow which follow which follow which follow follow follow follow follow follow follow follow follow follow. . . .

I choose to imitate and see.

So take him to your room and give him pillows. Let him throw the pillows at a wall. Let him shake them, let him stomp on them . . . stomp . . . stomp. . . .

STOMP ON THEM

stomp on them stomp on them stomp on them stomp on them stomp on them stomp on them stomp on them stomp on them stomp on them stomp on him stomp on him stomp on him stomp on him stomp on him stomp on him. . . .

I choose to imitate the life.

Because, beyond the discipline there is only danger and disorder. If we work eight hours, well, what then? Eight hours still remain before we sleep, and how are we to occupy ourselves . . . occupy ourselves . . . occupy ourselves . . .

OCCUPY OURSELVES

occupy ourselves occupy ourselves occupy ourselves occupy ourselves occupy ourselves occupy ourselves occupy ourselves occupy ourselves occupy ourselves occupy ourselves. . . .

What are we to do?

Imitate the life.

Sing together loudly for redemption.

Verbs with an originally short radical syllable . . . Ada, help me. Ada, please. . . .

Imitate the life and see.

Aren't you lonely all alone in that little house, Bucyrus?

You'll be lonelier and lonelier as years go by.

An old man needs a wife, that's sure Bucyrus.

He needs a helper, a companion — someone to grow old with . . . grow old with . . . to grow old with. . . .

OLD WITH

old with old with old with old with old with old with old with old with old with old with old with old with old with old with old with old with old with old with. . . .

And so you fornicated foully.

Ruining everything.

Breaking the pattern.

Right in my own house among my books and on my kitchen table: Raped me raped me raped me raped me raped me. . . .

RAPED ME

raped me raped me raped me raped me raped me raped me raped me raped me raped me raped me rape me rape me rape me rape me rapeme rapeme rapeme rapemerapeme rapemerapeme rapemerapemerapeme rapeme rapemerapemerapemerapeme. . . .

We'll judge, condemn, and damn the Beckey-slut.
We'll sing Bucyrus in the candle light and shadow.
We'll judge, condemn, and damn the Beckey-slut.
We'll sing Bucyrus in the candle light and shadow.

SHADOW SHADOW
shadow shadow shadow shadow shadow shadow shadow shadow shadow
SHADOW SHADOW

We'll hear revolting histories. Conceptions and our births.
We'll hear revolting histories. Conceptions and our births.
We'll hear revolting histories. Conceptions and our births.
Come rub my thighs.
Come rub my thighs.
Come rub my thighs, come kiss my cheeks.
Come rub my thighs, come kiss my cheeks.
Come rub my thighs.
Come rub my thighs, come kiss my cheeks.
Come rub my thighs, Come rub my thighs. Come rub my thighs. Come rub my thighs and rub my thighs and rub my thighs and rub my thighs and rub my thighs and rub my thighs and rub my thighs and rub my thighs and rub my thighs and rub my thighs and rub my thighs and rub my thighs and rub my thighs and rub my thighs and rub my thighs and rub my thighs and rub my thighs and rub my thighs and rub my thighs. . . .

COME KISS MY CHEEKS
THERE ARE SOME VERBS

III

for Peter Michelson

Statement

Once upon a time Ezra Pound, when he was still a young man, not so young he was still an imagist, but still young enough that he was a vorticist, once upon a time ol' Ez had him a friend called Gaudier-Brzeska. Now this Gaudier, this Gaudier-Brzeska who was a friend of Ezra Pound's (Pound the vorticist—always honoring craft) this Gaudier was a craftsman of genius—a sculptor. He worked on stone with his hands, and his hands were trained—*trained* hands. I mean the man knew what he did, didn't hack it with cudgels and hammers, didn't just kick it or punch it, he *sculpted* the stone with his exquisite perfectly trained controlled and controlling hands. (If, for example, the man had dug violin he would have taken the time to find out where one puts down one's fingers. If, for example, the man had dug the cooking of pastries, he would have learned from a pastry cook how to cook pastries. If, for example, the man had dug carpentry, he would have learned that screws hold under certain kinds of stresses where nails don't—etc. etc.) But his medium was stone. And he was a craftsman of genius—*of genius.* He had learned his craft, do you follow me. And that turned out (it does turn out, if you're serious, but most people aren't) to spell the difference between freedom and slavery, or, to be more precise in the parable, between freedom and imprisonment. "The instincts are not free springs of connation towards a goal. They are, so far as they can be abstractly separated, unconscious necessities, as Kant realized. They are unfree. But in their realisation as behaviour, when these innate things-in-themselves become things-for-themselves and interact with their environment (which also changes and is not the dead world of physics) they also change. Above all, they are changed in human culture. As a result of this change, these necessities become conscious, become emotion and thought; they exist for themselves and are altered thereby. The change *is* the emotion on thought, and now they are no longer the instincts, for they are conscious and consciousness is not an ethereal but a material determining relationship.

The necessity that is conscious is not the necessity that is unconscious. The conscious goal is different from the blind instinctive goal. It is freer." So then Gaudier. Gaudier choosing craft and consciousness, choosing freedom. So then Gaudier—Gaudier refusing to be enslaved by refusing to know, Gaudier refusing imprisonment. But they tried, the governments and their jailors, they tried, the governments and jailors unconscious and therefore unfree, to jail, in the war, this conscious spirit, this Gaudier. But Gaudier loved freedom, and because he loved freedom learned craft. Because he loved freedom learned craft so perfectly that he became a craftsman of genius. And his medium was stone. Stone were the jails of the governments and the jailors. Stone was his medium—a genius with exquisite perfectly trained controlled and controlling hands. Free hands. Free because they knew craft. Jails, Penitentiaries, Sanatoriums, all made out of stone. Stone walls, many feet thick. Stone jails. Jail-thick stone walls where they put him, craftsman and free, they—the governments making their wars.

Minutes after they threw him there in his cell, minutes after they locked him in that cage of stone, Gaudier, Pound's friend the vorticist, took, with his bare hands, an eight-foot-thick-wall apart and went home.

The Crazy Side of the Room

Nowhere to
be on
the crazy
side of
the room
     I was looking
     and looking
     for Ilya Petrovich
ah, for the wise and
ferocious loon of
a slav.
     Banging the giant
     whore nor plucking
     the harp was
     Ilya Petrovich; no, nor
     attending to who
     should attend the
     alchemical lectures.
I managed — which is
some consolation — to
find and engage in
philosophical chat
the obese and distinguished
Japanese violinist.
     Finally I said:
     where in
     the name
     of god is
     Petrovich?

     Gone at last
     to the wars?

Preface to Poem in Three Parts: One

(i)

Korok.

And of Korok, Kazi or Brelum
Teka or Tecta.

Libushka. Libushka
Of Korok, a sybil.

Weleska said: our lady
Libushka is dead.

But let us continue to rule.

(ii)

The tithes were refused.
The clergymen were assaulted.
Henry IV deferred to
The Bishop of Bremen.

Excommunicate (about '97)
And damned, the men
of that region deferred
To the women.

(iii)

Hordes of devils are making for France!
(The French, you know, are

a restless and turbulent people.)
Run the country in absence
of Husband and Son?
Libushka of Korok, a sybil.

(iv)

A toad the size of a goose or a duck.
The rhetoric of crusades.

Preface to Poem in Three Parts: Two
"Renaissance"

The knocked-up look is back!
(old accurate Van Eyck):
the turned-up pointed shoes,
the twin-peaked cap.
Gentlemen, there's no one
here but Gentlemen.

And Ladies.

And the Court.

Virgins of St. Denis
bare their privies for
the prince. And I am priest
and altar, consecrated host.
Bread and whiskey on
my loins, a wooden
phallus, nails:
I stiffen and endure.

Empty out the coffins, then.

Disinter the bones.

Preface to Poem in Three Parts: Three
   "Bull: (Vengence is mine)"

It has come to our ears that numbers of
both sexes do not avoid to have
intercourse

          and he said it has come to our ears

to have intercourse (fucking) with
incubi succubi demons on
saturday night / He was found in a posture!

Viz. On a stool by the hearth of the
chimney His feet on the floor His
body straight upward His shoulders
touching the lintel. And they by
their sorceries charm incantations
(and plagiaries) cause to expire
(extinguish) to perish (they suffocate!)
children of women increase of
animals corn of the ground grapes
of the vineyard fruit of the trees
as well as the men and the women
the flocks and the herds and all
other various kinds and kinds.

Viz. On a stool by the hearth.

Tied (his neck) with his
neck-cloth (whereof the
knot was behind) to a small
stick thrust in a hole in

the lintel. Having the strength
to bear the weight of
his body? his struggle?
Making procuring to blast
torment within and without.
That he could never have
been the actor himself. An
agent had done it: extraordinary, bizarre.

The door of the room was secured.

The human circle turns:

Widdershins.

Poem in Three Parts
Part One

(i)

wes cled in
a black gown
w/ a blak hat
vpon his

his faice was

his noise lyk

lyk the bek of ane egle gret bournyng

of an egle gret bournyng his eyn / His handis
and leggis wer herry His handis with clawes
His feit lyk / Wes cled in
vpon his

      Agnes Sampson

Agnes Sampson recording, official, brief: he had on
a gown and a hat which were both black. *Thank you.*
Thank you very much.

Agnes Sampson
Agnes Sharp
Agnes Stratton
Agnes Sparke

      Agnes Browne

Agnes Wobster

(Aberdeen: 1597)

Gentlemen

>   Somtym he vold be
>   lyk a stirk
>   lyk a bukk
>   lyk a rae
>   lyk a deir
>   lyk a dowg

>   He vold hold wp his taill

>   Lo! We kiss his arce.

Thank you.
Thank you very much.

and stript her there

a thing like
udder of a ewe
that giveth suck
two teats behind
her armhole there
her privie parts
and there as well
a teat a finger-length

and hairy
and

     Deliver me

They searched her body founde upon her cunt
a lump about the bigness of a nut and wett and
then they wrung it with their fingers there and
moisture came like lee . . .

(ii)

(a lantern there

or candle-light
I couldn't tell
a light a
phospherescence there
a presence
and

I danced

a sound of pleasant instruments
a violin and pipes
a tamborine
and singing there

around the great gray stone
and through the painted
gate obscured by fog

a semi-circle then
a circle formed
and Him astride
the first of us
inside

one by one inside that ring
he took

and markt them there

(iii)

in the kirk yard / with her daughters adoring

his member

          exceiding great and long / no manis
memberis so great and long / is abler for us then
than ony man could bee / is heavie lyk a stone and
verie cold as yce

      and stript her there

a thing like
udder of a ewe
that giveth suck

      abdoman 2
      fundament 3
      shoulder 1

pudenda 4

and under the arm

From which
familiars there
were wont to
suckle her . . .

Gentlemen:

(iv)

Gentlemen that gentleman
disappears in the East
cultivates beautiful manners
beautiful women
Engraves a heavy silver ring

                  with cabalistic signs

          Pious and elegant ladies

               there

    at the Alloway Kirk

(Father, confess me
for I am pretty and blonde.)

(Bagabi! Lamac! Samahac!
she didn't *say* she was twelve.

Didn't *say* she wanted to
cultivate beautiful manners.)

                    Reappears at Abbotsford

            told of
lonely roads: the others
walking in silence: a
bleating voice calling
from forest and plain.
(From the tips of her toes
to the crown of her head she
bathed herself with oil.
Then he took her quickly in the nave.)

Boredom? mainly.
(white monastic walls —
daughters there immured
and mortified)
boredom, mainly
leaden ennui
languid dreary melancholy days.

            Current of an inclination

                    imperceptible contagion

                            vaporous insinuation

        there

Tetanic immobility

Rigidity at first

Convulsionary epidemic in the end.

    Love

is license / All
the women his
Everybody manic or possessed.
In cities of renunciation
flagellants make law:
ecstasy makes criminals of girls.
Charges! Guilty!
(Fili Redemptor . . .)

       harden (oh, cannot) his hardest heart
Charges easy:
horny gods in trees:
every carnal field
a carnal synagogue
in May.
    Kobal! Nibbas!
Chancellor Adramaleck!
Emissaries, dignataries: post.

    Gentlemen, when exorcism fails,
    Drive along the highway to the coast.

I drove along the highway to the coast. Under sixty
all the while and looking sharp. I had memorized
directions; I had memorized my lines. I knew exactly
where to go and what I'd say. No pants. No bra.

I felt myself to be sure. I receited like a bull and
like a dog.   There was fog in patches and I
dimned the lights. Suddenly a lantern there ahead.
I parked by the side of the road and stared: rigid,
scared. Always this initial inclination to refuse.

       Always inclination

       Always to refuse

who said we shall (they did) assemble

(actual contemporaries)

shades.

The army told congressmen yesterday it has enough
of a single nerve gas in its chemical biological
warfare arsenal to kill the world's population
many times over. But Russia, one lawmaker reported,
may harbor an even more lethal capability in this
little discussed and highly secret field. The
substance is labeled by the army "G.B." and the
world's population is estimated at around 3.4 billion.
Rep. Robert L.F. Sikes, D-fla, said he thinks the
U.S. is not doing enough in the field. Sikes said
it is estimated the Russians have "seven to eight
times" the capability of the United States. The U.S.
has enough "G.B." to kill the world's estimated

population about 30 times. Russia, on the other hand,
has enough to kill the world's estimated population,

say

160 to 190 times.

Part Two

Pale and Black, unparfyt Whyte & Red, Pekoks
feathers (color gay) and Raynbow whych shall
overgoe the Spottyd Panther wyth the Lyon:

Croys byll
bloe
as lede:

F   e.s..   Rs & m.

A .   . E

f.m.   w.v.

W

m. .   m&m.

(Bird of Hermes
Goose of Hermogenes
Two-edged sword in the hand of the Cherub
    that guards the Tree of life,
        etc.)

76

o.g. − o.s. − q.
p.g. − p.s. − p.q.
s.s. − s.m. − s.s.
    *
    *
    *
    *
    *
    *
    *
    *
    *

        Mix and treat in
        philosopher's egg

           (one the
           Ram)

one the ram one the ram one the ram two the
bull one the ram two the bull three the twins
one the ram one the ram four the crab and the
lion and the virgin and the scales one the ram
one the ram and the scorpion and the archer and
the goat and aquarius twelve the fish one the
ram one the ram one the ram

       one the ram
       one the ram
       ten the goat
       four the crab
       two the bull

twelve the fish
one the ram

Visit the inward
parts of the earth,
by rectifying thou
shalt find

a picture of the sun
a picture of the moon

the keys
perhaps
of Basil Valentine

to whose major premise
we should reply.
to whose minor premise
we should reply.
to whom we must
respectfully submit.

And Oedipus said
to the Sphinx:

for a square of
the elements in
essence is
triangular

The hemisphere's

two lines are
straight and
curved.

(ii)

not until they died
because they mortified
not because they mortified they died
not because they died they mortified
not until they mortified
because they died

not homicide nor matricide nor suicide
infanticide nor fratricide deride
liquified and mollified and nullified
and petrified and purified replied
prophesied and glorified and rarefied
sanctified and rectified implied
classified and clarified and certified
typified personified allied
dignified and amplified and edified
modified and notified supplied
testified and satisfied and gratified
unified and villified espied
terrified and horrified and falsified
putrefied and ossified defied

not because they died because they mortified
because they mortified
until they died

(iii)

The Illuminated
Brotherhood of Avignon:
every last illuminated
brother lied. And
Paracelsus, Flamel, and
Agrippa lied.
Roger Bacon lied.
Albertus Magnus lied.

Gilles de Retz:
anticipating death
he told the
truth.

(iv)

the hieroglyphic figure
a dragon bites his tail
an emerald table and
the elemental sprite
the greater magistry
the humid path
the lesser magistry
the mystical drama of good
the composition of astra
the polarity of their molecules
the elements to which it belongs
the banner of Harpocrates
scion you congeal from 8 & 10
enigma & acrostic

the colors of the king
ubiquity of the end
primitive and proximate
the igneous principle there
the matrix of its acts
the value is 192
little cohesion draws
convex mirrors concave screens
a tingling metalline spirit
448, 344
an organ with seven pipes and an altar
rings on their fingers
swords with silver hilts
fine gay gloves on their hands
256, 224
to lie upon the primal waters
darkness of the world
a year in hiding or an influential friend
to undertake no study
the salt remains in the ash
the death of a man
the death, indeed, of a metal
take corporeal form
hidden by life
the severed heads of crows
a saffron-colored candle in the sky

such harmony / and yet this muddy vesture of decay

Whether the Canons were ever intended to be sung
whilst alchemical experiments were being carried
out cannot be determined with any degree of certainty.

The actual bearing of the words of the epigrams on
such experiments is by no means clear, as in no
case do they suggest invocation or incantation. It
is also difficult to believe that singers possessing
the necessary musical knowledge and experience could
be found amongst the laboratory assistants of the
time; it certainly would not be possible to find
                such assistants today

            matter, he said,
            expresses mysterious sound

            music coeval with speech

                number
                weight
                & measure

            chymic harps

(v)

    (Tripod over Flame) Doth not attempt to transmute
into gold but summon Thot o ibis-headed god o Mercury
(Tripod over Flame) Doth not attempt to transmute into
gold but summon Thot o ibis-
                    headed god o Mercury of
churning elements hermaphrodite (Tripod over Flame) Doth
not attempt to transmute into gold but summon Thot o
ibis-headed god o Mercury of churning elements

hermaphrodite and over hell in flask a
winged dragon call (Tripod over
Flame) Doth not attempt to
transmute into gold
but summon Thot o
ibis-headed
god
    o Mercury of churning elements hermaphrodite and
over hell in flask a winged dragon call doth not
attempt to transmute into gold (Tripod over Flame)
doth not attempt to transmute into gold is no vain
cauldron-cook or chemist but for Thot will sweat
        whole days and nights before that
           furnace until face explode in boils
             and running sores (Tripod over Flame)
               doth not attempt to transmute into gold is
                  no vain cauldron-cook or chemist but for Thot
will sweat whole days and nights
before that furnace until face
explode in boils and running
sores his fingers burn in
coals & clay & filth to
summon Thot o ibis-headed
god o Mercury of churning
elements hermaphrodite
and over hell

in flask

a winged dragon

call

                         (which shall be a sign unto you)

(vi)

sublimation
amalgamation
calcination
         (ascension
         fixation)
rubification
albification
         (ceration)

coagulation
imbibation
incorporation
citrination
         (cementing)

fermentation
inollification
induration
         (ablution)
mortification
mortification
Thot

sublimation amalgamation calcination
rubification albification coagulation
imbibation incorporation citrination

fermentation inollification induration
mortification mortification mortification
THOT.

                    pot tobreketh / al is go

                    Hermes Trismegistos, where?

(vii)

Sing-bonga, angered
by the smoke, sent
crows. Later he slept
in the furnace.

Sing-anga, earlier
and far away, a
fetus found and
burned:
        "on that ash
        erect a temple, Yakut shaman."

Yang & Yin
Yin & Yang

For the smith
and his bride,
these coals.

(viii)

could boil,
melt

(ego in
      hand)
his world.

therefore feared
as agent
      ("public
      menace")

matter unre-
generate
mirrors
(crime).

Verbum dictum factum: god in
the vowels of the earth:

ascribe unto
these metals,
Hermes,
need.

(ix)

(otherwise
perceive the imperfection
understand

not to imperfection
even otherwise
command

dross & refuse &
decay

ascend
condense)

Philosophy, he held, was out of hand.

(x)

Whether C. was
        duped "per doctrinam"
Whether C. knew
        Shuchirch at all

        William de Brumley, 'chaplain lately
dwelling with the Prior of Harmandsworth' —
does he lie?

Whether C was a
victim or student . . .

                (hermaphroditic rebis
                there appeared.

                Probably not.)

                Probably not.

                later,
                after

(xi)

The still-providing
world is not
enough: we add.

Ponder matter
where impatient
sleepers wait.

And Aphrodite
saw her soul
was stone.

And Nargajuna
dreamed that
he was glad.

Part Three

save and except the area described
as follows:

> beginning at the southwest
> corner of the Atlantic Beach
> on the Atlantic Ocean (the
> southeast corner of the property
> known as the Hoffman Property)
> thence running westwardly with
> the Atlantic Ocean waters to
> a point on the ocean two miles
> from the beginning thence northwardly
> and parallel with the west line of
> the Atlantic Beach to the waters
> of Bogue Sound to the
> northwest corner of the Atlantic
> Beach thence with that line
> which is the east line of the
> Hoffman property to the beginning

Save and Except.
Save and Except these lands.
Preserve the Saltar Path.
Alice Hoffman not allowed on
the Saltar Path. Saltar Path
no property of Alice Hoffman.

> Kitty Hawk
> Albermale Sound
> Manteo
> Roanoke Island
> Hatteras

Cape Hatteras
Ocracoke Island
Pamlico Sound
Portsmouth Island
Core Banks
Shackleford Banks
Bogue Banks

approached by sea how
long ago, Davy
John Willis?

Robert Sullivan writes,
circa 1943: "I'd rather go to court than to the theatre."
Thus Mrs. H., circa 1943.

Durham
Raleigh
Goldsboro
New Bern
Morehead City
Beaufort
Bogue Banks

"Beaufort"
"Bowfut"
"Beeoofud"
Bogue Banks

North Carolina for the North Carolinians; Bogue
Banks for the Bankers.

(1)   *Storm after storm:*
        we cannot any longer
        hold this course: storm
        after storm: Hatteras,
        Cape Hatteras, Shackleford
        Banks: storm after storm:
        food gone: water gone:
        men near mutiny: we
        cannot any longer
        hold this course:
        Hatteras, Cape Hatteras,
        Shackleford Banks . . .

                OUTPOST OF ISOLATION
                300 YEARS 300 YEARS
                SQUATTERS ON N.CAROLINA
                SANDBANK THREATEN VIOLENCE

(2)   Through groves of
        twisted yaupon trees
        to the beach . . . a morning
        and an evening haul . . .
        barefoot on the sand
        and singing, singing . . .
        Settlers driven out
        of Shackleford by
        drifting dunes, out
        of Diamond city . . .
        Gardens would not
        grow in the sand,
        cattle could not
        graze, so back (how

many years, John Willis?)
to the sea.

OUTPOST OF ISOLATION
300 YEARS 300 YEARS
SQUATTERS ON N.CAROLINA
SANDBANK THREATEN VIOLENCE

(3)   Formal gardens, cultivated
lawns, fountains, arbours,
fancy foreign friends. Once
she brought a harpsichord
from France. Who's the law?
Judge A. Flint. *He* lived a long
time ago. And here we are off
Morehead City Bridge.
Shackleford was sold to the
state, Bogue was sold to
the army. Now we've got
Fort Macon and a
missile base . . .

Did they murder the cooks? Hack
the Butler up? Did they
drink the blood of
the maids?

solid world / measure incomplete

ends and beginnings
cannot be regarded
as fixed

beginning at the southwest
corner of the Atlantic Beach

92

on the Atlantic Ocean (the
southeast corner of the property
known as the Hoffman Property)
thence running westwardly with
the Atlantic Ocean waters to
a point on the ocean two miles
from the beginning thence northwardly
and parallel with the west line of
the Atlantic Beach to the waters
of Bogue Sound to the
northwest corner of the Atlantic
Beach thence with that line
which is the east line of the
Hoffman Property to the beginning

it is understood and agreed and made a part of this judgement that
neither of the parties hereto will interfere in any way with the
full exercise of the rights of the other as adjudicated in this
instrument and that each of said parties shall be entitled to
exercise their rights or privileges as the case may be without
interference on the part of the other . . .

Thus the Judge . . .
and under his
breath:
        'In the
solid world
measurements
are incomplete.
Time has no
stopping, divisions
have no permanance
and ends and be-

ginnings have no
fixity. The man
of great wisdom
observes both
far and near,
not thinking of
what is large,
knowing that
measurements are
incomplete. He
is aware of both
fullness and
emptiness so that
he neither rejoices
at life nor thinks
of death as calamity
knowing that ends
and beginnings
cannot be
regarded
as fixed . . .

(save and except the area described
as follows)

beginning at the southwest
corner of the Atlantic Beach
on the Atlantic Ocean (the
southeast corner of the property
known as the Hoffman property)

men with torches knives and other
implements of butchery destruction
desecration did intent on violence
thence run westwardly with Ocean
waters to a point on Ocean sands
two miles from beginning and thence
northwardly and parallel with
West Line of Atlantic to the
waters of the Bogue and thence
with waters of the Bogue to
northwest corner of Atlantic
Beach and thence along that
line to the beginning and did
terrorize the titled lady
living there (said Mrs. H.) did
sack the land did burn the
mansion to the ground did
rape and ravish slaughter and
profane did catch the chauffeur
cut away his genitals did murder cooks
did hack the butler up did drink
the blood of pink Parisian maids . . .

                                BUT

This cause coming on to be heard and being
heard by the court and a jury, the court having
instructed the jury that there was
                        NO EVIDENCE
                        NO EVIDENCE

Across Bogue Sound
The Tar-Heels
Saw a Castle
Rise.

Fires there, and
each man with a
torch. Crazy through
the houses
scattered round
the backbone of
the bank. Crazy
up the island nob
and down the
Saltar Path through
underbrush and
over dunes and
under over-
hanging limbs

Across Bogue Sound
The Tar-Heels
Saw a Jungle
Blaze.

Did they murder the cooks? Hack
the Butler up? Did they
drink the blood of
the maids?

solid world / measure incomplete

                    ends and beginnings
                    cannot be regarded
                    as fixed

. . . whereas there is now pending
in the district court of the United States
an action entitled
United States against 735 acres of land
more or less

Davy John Willis
sits on the beach
and mends nets.

Remembers little.

His ancestors were
pirates.

                    Mrs. H.
was afraid of him
and of coral snakes . . .

                              and of the jungle
                              and of the swamps
                              and of mosquitoes . . .

          (dunes drift, the

sand covers
the crops . . .

And you have been here?
Three Hundred Years.
And your people?
Fish in the sea.

"Bucyrus" makes use of seven short quotes each from James W. Bright's *Anglo-Saxon Reader* and Richard Baxter's *The Saints Everlasting Rest* as well as certain statements attributed to L. Ron Hubbard in an article on Scientology published in *Life* magazine some five or so years ago. The quotation in "Statement" is from Christopher Caudwell's *The Concept of Freedom*. "Preface to Poem in Three Parts: One" derives from Chapters 3, 5, and 12 of Julio Caro Baroja's *The World of the Witches*. "Preface to Poem in Three Parts: Two" derives from Chapter 13 of Jules Michelet's *Satanism and Witchcraft*. "Preface to Poem in Three Parts: Three" is a found poem with grafts linking the 1484 Bull of Pope Innocent VIII with John Reid's testimony as given in *Narrative of the Sufferings of a Young Girle*. Part One of "Poem in Three Parts" takes testimony and narrative from Margaret A. Murray's *The Witch-Cult in Western Europe*, narrative and commentary from *Satanism and Witchcraft* and from Kurt Seligmann's *The History of Magic,* and occasional details from Jean Lhermitte's *True and False Possession*. The concluding prose paragraph is from United Press International. Though the formulae in Part Two of "Poem in Three Parts" come from a number of primary sources (Paracelsus, Basil Valentine, Roger Bacon, Petrus Bonus, Albertus Magnus, Cornelius Agrippa, Norton, Asmole, Ripley, etc.) my immediate source was usually John Read's *Prelude to Chemistry*. For interpretation I have drawn most heavily on Jung's "The Idea of Redemption in Alchemy" from *The Integration of the Personality*. Frederic Spiegleberg's *Alchemy as a Way of Salvation,* and my own *Th' Entencioun and Speche of Philosophres* (unpublished). The prose paragraph beginning "Whether the canons were ever intended to be sung . . ." is from F.H. Sawyer's "The Music in 'Atalanta Fugiens,' " printed as an appendix in Read. Part Three of "Poem in Three Parts" gets its law from Henry L. Stevens, Jr., Presiding Judge in the Superior Court of Carteret County, North Carolina, 1944: *Mrs. Alice Hoffman and Bogue Banks, Incorporated* vs. *Llewellyn Phillips and John Marshall Matthias, Trustee, The Alden Corporation and R.N. Larrimer*. It gets its philosophy from Chuang Tz out of Derek Wavell's "Belinda File," and some of its incidents and details from an article by Robert Sullivan in the *Sunday News* (Oct. 7, 1945) and from accounts given me over the years by my parents—who were there. Other writings from which I have profitted in a general way during the composition of these concluding collages include: Emile Durkheim, *The Elementary Forms of the Religious Life;* Paul Christian, *The History and Practice of Magic;* John Middleton, ed., *Magic, Witchcraft, and Curing;* Jacobus Sprenger and Heinrich Kramer, *Malleus Maleficarum;* Max Marwick, ed., *Witchcraft and Sorcery;* Pennethorne Hughes, *Witchcraft;* A.E. Waite, ed., *The Hermetic Museum* and *The Hermetic and Alchemical Writings of Paracelsus;* M. Caron and S. Hutin, *The Alchemists.*